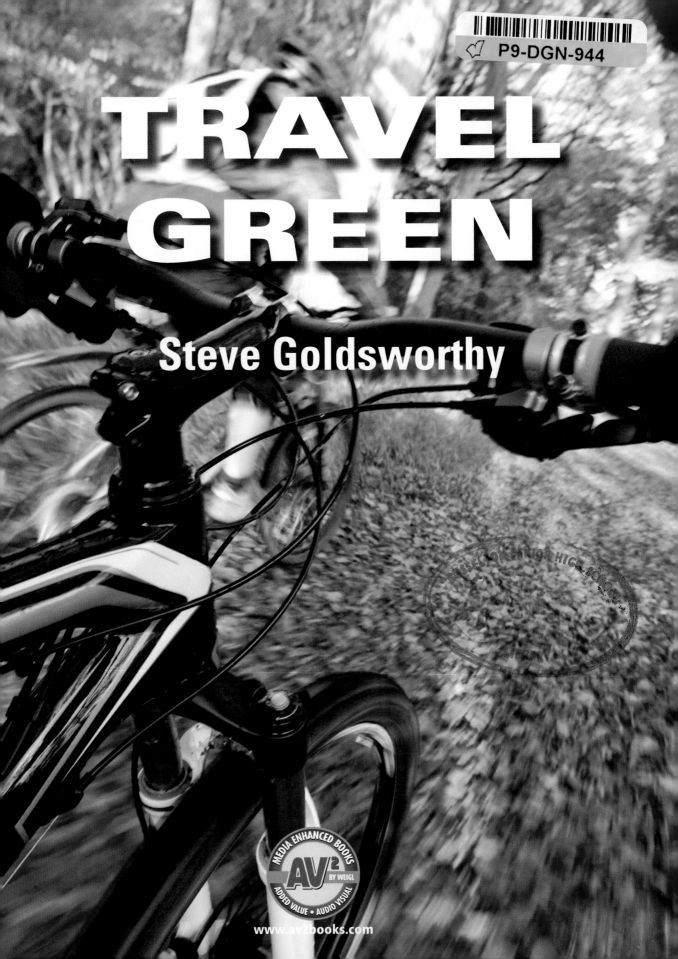

TRAVEL GREEN

Steve Goldsworthy

MEDIA ENHANCED BOOKS
AV2 BY WEIGL
ADDED VALUE • AUDIO VISUAL

www.av2books.com

AV² by Weigl brings you media enhanced books that support active learning.

AV² provides enriched content that supplements and complements this book. Weigl's AV² books strive to create inspired learning and engage young minds for a total learning experience.

Go to **www.av2books.com**, and enter this book's unique code. You will have access to video, audio, web links, quizzes, a slide show, and activities.

BOOK CODE

L305863

Audio
Listen to sections of the book read aloud.

Video

Web Link
Find research sites and play interactive games.

Try This!
Complete activities and hands-on experiments.

Due to the dynamic nature of the Internet, some of the URLs and activities provided as part of AV² by Weigl may have changed or ceased to exist. AV² by Weigl accepts no responsibility for any such changes. All media enhanced books are regularly monitored to update addresses and sites in a timely manner. Contact AV² by Weigl at 1-866-649-3445 or av2books@weigl.com with any questions, comments, or feedback.

Published by AV² by Weigl
350 5th Avenue, 59th Floor
New York, NY 10118
Web site: www.av2books.com   www.weigl.com

Library of Congress Cataloging-in-Publication Data available upon request.
Fax 1-866-44-WEIGL for the attention of the Publishing Records department.

ISBN 978-1-61690-085-4 (hard cover)
ISBN 978-1-61690-086-1 (soft cover)

Printed in the United States of America in North Mankato, Minnesota
1 2 3 4 5 6 7 8 9 0 14 13 12 11 10

062010
WEP264000

Project Coordinators: Heather C. Hudak, Robert Famighetti
Design: Terry Paulhus
Project Editor: Emily Dolbear
Photo Research: Edward A. Thomas
Layout and Production: Tammy West

Every reasonable effort has been made to trace ownership and to obtain permission to reprint copyright material. The publishers would be pleased to have any errors or omissions brought to their attention so that they may be corrected in subsequent printings.

Weigl acknowledges Getty Images as its primary image supplier for this title.

CONTENTS

MAKING THE WORLD A GREENER PLACE

How can you make the world a greener place? You can help the planet by reducing your **carbon footprint**. A carbon footprint is the measure of **greenhouse gases** produced by human activities.

Greenhouse gases are produced by burning **fossil fuels**. People burn fossil fuels for electricity, heating, and powering vehicles. One of the biggest causes of climate change is the greenhouse gas known as **carbon dioxide**. Many scientists believe that carbon **emissions** are more damaging to Earth than any other kind of pollution.

There are many ways you can reduce your carbon footprint. One way is to walk or ride your bike instead of riding in a car. You can turn off lights when you leave a room to reduce energy waste. Reusing plastic shopping bags to carry other items is another way to help the environment. You can **recycle** newspaper so that fewer trees are chopped down to make new paper.

HOW CAN YOU TRAVEL GREEN?

Traveling green is one way to help keep your world green. Think about your daily travel. How do you get to school? Do you travel by bus or car, or do you walk? Where does your family vacation? Do you choose a far-off destination or take day trips? Do you travel by car, plane, train, or boat? How do you travel when you arrive at your destination?

A HISTORY OF GREEN
TRAVEL

To plan for the future, people must sometimes look to the past. Humankind has a long history of green travel. Before cars, buses, and trains, there were many kinds of transportation that caused less harm to the environment.

WAYS PEOPLE TRAVELED GREEN IN THE PAST

Used Wheels

Wagons with wheels date back more than 5,500 years. The people who lived in what is now Iraq were likely the first people to use wagons. The spoked wheel, invented some time after, led to the development of lighter, swifter wheeled vehicles. The Greeks introduced chariot racing in 680 BC. The Romans also adopted the sport.

> "Honor the sacred. Honor the Earth, our Mother."
> –*American Indian proverb*

Rode Human-Powered Vehicles

A German baron invented an early two-wheeled human-powered vehicle in about 1817. Like a scooter, the vehicle had no pedals. The driver pushed along with his or her feet and then coasted. The vehicle was mainly wood, with iron wheels and a rear-wheel brake. The two-wheeled machine went through several improvements, including the pedal-powered bicycle with a huge front wheel. J. K. Starley produced a prototype of the modern-day bicycle in 1885. It featured two wheels of equal size.

Floated Rivers, canals, and other waterways have always provided a way to transport goods and travel. Barges are still in use today. In the past, a barge driver used a pole in the water or towed the barge from the riverbank with a horse or ox. American Indians traveled by canoe for thousands of years before European explorers and fur traders did the same in the 16th and 17th centuries.

2 GREEN CARS

O ne of the biggest contributors to greenhouse gas emissions is the automobile. Today, more than 250 million vehicles are on the road in the United States. Transportation fuels are the second leading cause of greenhouse gas emissions by humans. U.S. vehicles are responsible for almost half of all **global warming** linked to cars. Many greener alternatives exist.

WAYS TO BECOME ECO-FRIENDLY DRIVERS

Look for a Fuel-Efficient Car

Look at a car's fuel efficiency. How many miles (kilometers) can it travel per gallon (liter) of gas? The higher the fuel efficiency, the less gas the car consumes to travel the same distance. Of course, smaller cars are more efficient than bigger vehicles. Two-door and four-door compact cars get better gas mileage than trucks, minivans, or sport utility vehicles (SUVs), though they cannot carry as many people or as much cargo. Motorbikes and scooters use even less fuel. Does your family have a car? What is its fuel efficiency?

Drive an Electric Car

Although electric cars have existed almost as long as gas-fueled cars, these vehicles are more expensive to make. Today's electric cars also have big electric batteries that require charging. An electric car, such as the Nissan LEAF, plugs into a refueling station or even a home garage outlet. However, electric cars still require energy to run. In many cases, the electricity comes from coal-burning electricity-generating plants, which pollute the atmosphere. Some electricity-generating plants, however, use hydropower or wind power. Both of these sources are environmentally friendly.

Buy a Hybrid

Hybrids are a type of green car. A hybrid car usually runs on two different power sources—a gasoline engine and an electric motor. Most major car manufacturers produce some form of gas-electric car. Many of these vehicles use an electric motor for speeds of less than 35 miles (55 kilometers) per hour. When the car speeds up, the gasoline engine provides additional power. This allows the car to run on electricity on city streets and mostly on gas for highway driving. How much gas do you think a hybrid vehicle would save the average driver?

3 OTHER GREEN VEHICLES

The world has many vehicles in addition to automobiles. Trains, airplanes, ships, and motorcycles also contribute to greenhouse gas emissions. Scientists and engineers are working hard to make these forms of transportation greener.

WAYS TO TRAVEL GREEN USING DIFFERENT TYPES OF VEHICLES

Ride on Electric Trains
Cities and towns all over the world use electric trains for public transit. One type of electric train is called a third rail train. It travels on two rails and gets electricity to power its motor from a third rail. An overhead-system train gets its electricity through a device that runs along a wire above the train tracks. A **monorail** train moves on a single rail that gives the train its power. Electric trains are often faster than traditional diesel-fueled trains. They produce no pollution and run quietly.

Pedal an Electric Bicycle
China is the world's leading producer of electric bicycles. Electric bicycles account for up to 20 percent of the country's two-wheeled vehicles. An electric motor powers the vehicle or assists with pedaling. While electric bicycles do not rely on plug-in electricity, they use batteries. Batteries are often manufactured and disposed of in ways that are not environmentally friendly.

Sail on Solar Power
PlanetSolar, with its 328 solar panels, is the world's biggest boat powered by the Sun. The goal of the boat's German owners was to build a vessel capable of sailing around the globe using **renewable** energy. However, the boat was very expensive to build. It cost more than $24 million.

"When we heal the earth, we heal ourselves."
–*David Orr, environmental educator and writer*

4 GREENER FUELS

Fossil fuels are formed over millions of years from plant and animal remains. They include coal, natural gas, and oil. Burning fossil fuels contributes to global warming. Did you know that coal produces more carbon dioxide per **megajoule** than any other fossil fuel? The world's supply of fossil fuels is running out. Using green fuel is one solution.

GREENER WAYS TO FUEL VEHICLES

Use Renewable Energy

Renewable energy sources include wind power, solar power, and water power. They are excellent alternatives to coal for generating electricity for hybrid and electric vehicles. Scientists are working hard to expand the capabilities of wind farms, **hydroelectric** dams, and solar panels. Do some research to find out if your community has renewable energy sources.

> "I'd put my money on the sun and solar energy. What a source of power! I hope we don't have to wait till oil and coal run out before we tackle that."
>
> —*Thomas Edison, American inventor, 1931*

Fuel with Biofuels

Today, some vehicles can run on renewable fuels called **biofuels**. Bioethanol is alcohol made from the sugars of sugarcane, corn, or potatoes. Biodiesel is made from recycled grease, animal fat, or vegetable oil. Scientists can even make usable fuel from livestock manure.

Drive a Solar Vehicle

Solar vehicles once existed only in science fiction. Today, Sun-powered cars, bicycles, planes, and boats are becoming reality. Every two years, universities across the United States and Canada participate in a race called the North American Solar Challenge. Science and engineering students design, build, and race solar cars across the continent in a week-long competition. Covered with solar panels, these vehicles convert sunlight directly into electricity. There is even a solar vehicle competition for high school students.

5 TRAVELING GREEN
LOCALLY

Every day, people go to school, visit the park or library, shop, and work. Think about how many miles (kilometers) are covered in a day, a week, and a month. Then, multiply that number by the number of people living in a certain area. All those miles (kilometers) add up. Every trip a person takes, no matter how short, is a chance to travel green.

WAYS TO TRAVEL GREEN IN YOUR COMMUNITY

Bike Biking is an excellent way to travel green. Start with a well-maintained bike that fits you properly. It should have a bell, lights, and a water-bottle holder. You may want a carrier for supplies. Many people can cycle at about 15 miles (24 km) per hour. If you had an hour to bike, where could you go?

"We do not inherit the earth from our ancestors, we borrow it from our children."
–*American Indian proverb*

Carpool When unrelated people ride in one car, they are carpooling. Carpooling is becoming more popular in and around cities. Most carpoolers take turns driving a group of people to school or work. This system reduces the cost of fuel for each participant, as well as overall fuel use. Fewer cars on the road also means less fuel is used and fewer greenhouse gases are emitted.

Use Mass Transit Public mass transit includes buses, aboveground trains, subways, and ferries. Some mass transit uses renewable energy, such as biofuel buses. This makes it even greener. Mass transit is especially effective in heavily populated areas. For example, the New York City subway system, which averages more than five million passengers each weekday, is one of the busiest in the world. How often do you use mass transit? The next time you are on a bus, train, subway, or ferry, count the passengers and calculate how many car trips have been saved by riding transit.

PLANNING FOR GREEN
TRAVEL

6

It is not just the type of vehicle or the fuel used that people should consider when traveling green. All trips require careful planning, especially if you are trying to travel green. What will you take on your trip? How will you eat? What impact will your visit have on the environment? These are some of the questions to consider when traveling green.

WAYS TO PREPARE FOR TRAVELING GREEN

Pack Light Packing light is always the greenest way to travel. An extra 100 pounds (45 kilograms) of luggage can decrease your vehicle's fuel efficiency by up to two percent. In addition, every 1 mile (1.6 km) over a speed limit of 55 miles (90 km) per hour can lower a car's fuel efficiency by almost two percent.

Make Meals Without Litter

Consider making meals that leave no litter when you travel. Avoid packaged or boxed foods. Processed items are not as healthful as fresh, unpackaged food, and much of the garbage they generate is not recycled. Make as much of your food from scratch as possible. Use small resealable containers with airtight lids to store food. What other ways can you think of to take your favorite foods while still traveling green?

"Take nothing but pictures. Leave nothing but footprints. Kill nothing but time."

–Motto of the Baltimore Grotto, a Maryland caving society

Visit with Respect Camping trips require special research. Respect nature, especially if you are traveling into a natural area. Most people know not to litter or feed animals. Check with park rangers, tour guides, or other local people about hazards related to the weather, the season, and wildlife. Be aware of how your presence affects the environment. Stay away from any signs of animal mothers and their young. Do not disturb nests, burrows, or dens even if they look abandoned. Remain on the hiking trails to avoid damaging plant life.

7 GREEN VACATIONS

There are many destinations to choose from when traveling green. People need to consider carefully where they want to go and how they plan to get there. Many travel agents offer special "green vacations." They will help travelers pick a destination, make a green plan for getting there, and organize eco-friendly activities.

WAYS TO VACATION GREEN

Go Local Traveling locally is the simplest, most cost-effective way to vacation green. Traveling to a nearby town by car or mass transit cuts down on greenhouse gases. It may even be possible to reach certain destinations by biking or walking.

"There are no passengers on Spaceship Earth. We are all crew."
–*Marshall McLuhan, Canadian educator*

Do What You Do at Home

If you stay in a hotel on vacation, remember to think green. Use the hotel's recycling program. Try to stay in hotels that save water with low-flush toilets, use motion sensors to turn off lights in the bathroom, and have low-energy light bulbs. Reuse towels to save on laundry detergent and the water needed to wash them. Turn off the heat or air-conditioning and all lights when you leave the room.

Pick a central location so you can walk to the places you plan to visit. Find a bike to rent or use public transportation to explore. What else could you do in a hotel to stay green?

Take a Working Vacation

One way to travel green is to take a working vacation. Tour guides lead tree-planting vacations in Canada, South America, or Thailand. You can experience diverse cultures and lend a hand with **reforestation**. On a working farm vacation in England, for example, people get room and board in a country cottage in exchange for helping out with farm work. Travelers learn how to tend sheep, weed gardens, and harvest vegetables. What kind of working vacation interests you?

8 GREEN DESTINATIONS

What makes a destination green? Green destinations have programs to reduce greenhouse gas emissions, restore natural areas, and protect wildlife. Traveling to faraway destinations is not green, however. If you must fly to reach your destination, consider buying **carbon offsets**. These are credits that reduce the buyer's carbon footprint by supporting green projects, such as reforestation.

WAYS TO VACATION IN GREEN DESTINATIONS

See the Greenest City

Many of the world's environmental groups rate Reykjavik, the capital city of Iceland, the world's greenest city. The North Atlantic Ocean island of Iceland has abundant water and volcanic activity, so Reykjavik gets much of its energy from renewable resources. Houses are often heated with **geothermal energy**. The city uses hydrogen-powered buses. These vehicles produce no carbon dioxide, and only water is emitted from their tailpipes. However, hydrogen fuel is difficult to make and store.

Bike Through a City Portland, Oregon, has the largest wilderness park within the limits of a U.S. city. About eight percent of Portland residents bike to work regularly. That is more than any other major city in the country. Portland was the first U.S. city to adopt a Global Warming Action Plan. The city's Urban Greenspaces Institute works to develop harmony between the natural environment and buildings, parks, and trails. What green initiatives does your community have?

"A journey of a thousand miles must begin with a single step."
–Lao-tzu, Chinese philosopher

View Wildlife The African nation of Kenya has worked to protect its wildlife and improve its **sustainability** for decades. In Mombasa, the government is building Hacienda.

This is a self-sustained community with renewable power sources and an agricultural system to feed its residents. The Kenya Wildlife Service, established in 1990, oversees 35 designated national parks and preserves. Park admission fees are used to protect wildlife. The service runs forest and wetland conservation programs and partners with local communities to conserve natural resources.

9 TRAVEL GREEN, TRAVEL HEALTHY

When you choose to travel green, you are making a healthful choice for the planet and also for yourself. Think of all the ways you can travel with the power of your own body. You can walk, jog, or bike to get places. You can canoe or kayak. You can skate or ski. It can be rewarding to know you are taking care of yourself, as well as the environment around you.

WAYS TRAVELING GREEN KEEPS YOU HEALTHY

Get More Exercise

One of the greenest ways to travel is walking. Exercise helps strengthen your heart and other muscles. It can also help you lose extra body weight. A person can walk for 30 minutes and burn about 80 calories. A brisk two-hour hike can burn 500 calories. A two-hour bike ride of 20 miles (32 km) will burn more than 700 calories. How can you get more exercise by traveling green?

Relieve Stress

Walking to school or riding your bike to the movies does not add to greenhouse emissions. It can also help relieve stress. Exercising can decrease the production of stress hormones. Consider taking walks regularly with a friend or joining a sports group to make walking or biking a healthful habit for your body and mind.

Breathe Better

Studies have shown that air travel generates at least 600 million tons (544 million metric tons) of carbon dioxide each year. The average car produces about 12,000 pounds (5,440 kg) of carbon dioxide a year. Greener forms of transportation put much less carbon dioxide into the air. One of the biggest benefits to the environment from traveling green is better air quality. Cleaner air means people and animals can breathe better.

"Take care of the earth and she will take care of you." *–Unknown*

10 GREEN TRAVEL IN THE FUTURE

Many trips that take hours today would have required weeks or months 100 years ago. It is easy to hop aboard an airplane without thinking about the miracle of flight or the environmental impact of the trip. What will green travel look like in the future? What technological advances will engineers and scientists make in this field?

WAYS TO TRAVEL GREEN IN THE FUTURE

Use a Podcar

One alternative to buses, trains, and other public transportation is the personal automated transport (PAT), or **podcar**. The small podcar would run on a train track. Instead of stopping at every station to load and unload passengers, the podcar would go directly to your station. Podcars would run on renewable energy sources. What are some advantages to podcars? What are some disadvantages?

> "Speed is irrelevant if you are going in the wrong direction."
> –*Indian leader Mahatma Gandhi (1869–1948)*

Ride on More Efficient Trains

Many people hope that high-speed trains will rival the speed of planes one day. In Japan, every year, six billion passengers ride the train daily. On the Shinkansen line, the bullet train has an average speed of 180 miles (300 km) per hour. France's Trains à Grande Vitesse (TGVs) are already some of the world's fastest electric trains. Engineers are researching more efficient forms of renewable energy, including geothermal energy, to power trains. They are also looking for ways to build more tunnels to create direct routes. As the planet's population grows, what travel needs will people have? How will they travel green?

Travel by Airship and Spaceship

Airships, or **dirigibles**, date back to the late 1700s. Airships are mostly used by companies, not passengers. However, designs are being developed for faster, greener airships. In addition, advances have been made in fuel usage. Airships, as well as regular airplanes, are experimenting with adjustable solar panels that fuel electric motors. At some point in the future, people might be able to visit space stations, the Moon, or even Mars using spaceships powered by solar power. What do you think is the future of flight?

Carbon Dioxide Emissions for Car, Train, and Airplane Travel

Carbon Dioxide Produced per 100 miles (160 km)*:

For a typical car:
about 71 pounds (32 kg)

For a train passenger:
about 6.5 pounds (2.9 kg)

For an airplane passenger:
about 30–70 pounds (14–32 kg)

*These are estimates. A vehicle's size and speed, the number of passengers, and the type of fuel used can affect the amount of carbon dioxide produced per passenger mile (kilometer).

CARBON DIOXIDE PRODUCED FOR THREE TRIPS BY CAR

① **Chicago to New York City**
795 miles (1,279 km)
568 pounds (258 kg) of carbon dioxide produced

② **Dallas to New Orleans**
519 miles (835 km)
371 pounds (168 kg) of carbon dioxide produced

③ **Denver to Las Vegas**
766 miles (1,233 km)
547 pounds (248 kg) of carbon dioxide produced

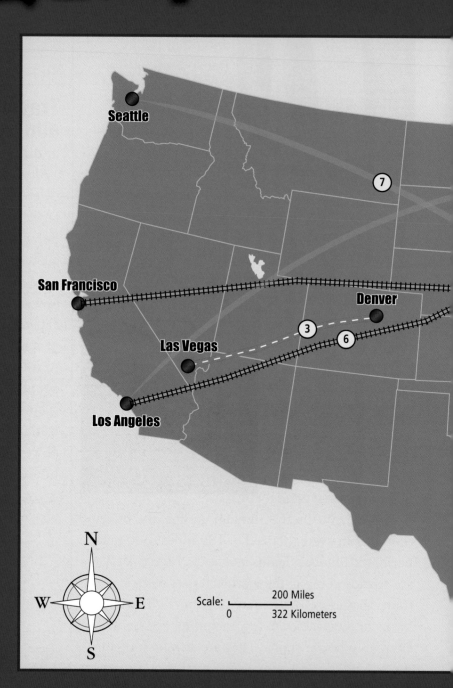

Vehicles that run on fossil fuels produce carbon dioxide, measured in pounds (kilograms) per mile (kilometer). Compare modes of transportation to determine the best way to travel green.

CARBON DIOXIDE PRODUCED FOR THREE TRIPS BY TRAIN, PER PASSENGER

4 **New York City to San Francisco**
3,397 miles (5,467 km)
220 pounds (100 kg) of carbon dioxide produced

5 **New York City to New Orleans**
1,377 miles (2,216 km)
88 pounds (40 kg) of carbon dioxide produced

6 **Chicago to Los Angeles**
2,256 miles (3,630 km)
144 pounds (65 kg) of carbon dioxide produced

CARBON DIOXIDE PRODUCED FOR THREE TRIPS BY AIRPLANE, PER PASSENGER

7 **Seattle to Orlando**
2,546 miles (4,097 km)
815 pounds (370 kg) of carbon dioxide produced

8 **Washington, D.C. to Boston**
393 miles (632 km)
265 pounds (120 kg) of carbon dioxide produced

9 **New York City to Los Angeles**
2,451 miles (3,945 km)
794 pounds (360 kg) of carbon dioxide produced

Legend
Car
Train
Airplane
City

GreenCareers

Innovation comes from people asking questions. People working in the field of green technology often ask, "How do we make this world a greener place?"

Transportation Design Engineer

Career

One of the most exciting jobs in green travel is designing new vehicles. It takes creativity and knowledge in many disciplines to create and manufacture attractive, eco-friendly motorcycles, automobiles, buses, and trucks. Transportation design engineers must strike a green balance between the needs of consumers and the environment.

Education

Transportation design engineers study technical drawing, drafting, mechanics, electronics, and environmental design at a college or university. They have at least a bachelor's degree and, in many cases, a graduate degree.

Transportation Planner

Career

Transportation planner is a challenging but rewarding job. These highly skilled professionals must have knowledge in many fields. They plan public transportation for cities. They are informed about all available trains, buses, and other vehicles, as well as renewable power sources for these vehicles. Transportation planners set policies for these services. In Portland, Oregon, transportation planners designed options for downtown commuters, including the Free Rail Zone, where anyone can ride the light rail system and streetcars. This initiative encourages people to use public transportation, cutting down on congestion and pollution. Transportation planners must be creative in solving challenges.

Education

Transportation planners are often civil engineers. This field requires study in mathematics, economics, and the physical sciences.

What have you learned about Traveling Green?

Are you a green travel expert?
Take this quiz to test your knowledge.

1 What U.S. city was the first to adopt a Global Warming Action Plan?

2 What are examples of fossil fuels?

3 What is a hybrid car?

4 Which fossil fuel produces the most carbon dioxide per megajoule?

5 How many passengers does the New York City subway system average each weekday?

6 How much can an extra 100 pounds (45 kg) of luggage decrease your vehicle's fuel efficiency?

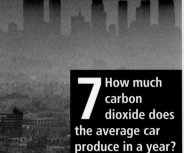

7 How much carbon dioxide does the average car produce in a year?

8 What does PAT stand for?

ANSWERS: 1. Portland, Oregon **2.** Coal, gas, and oil **3.** A car that uses a gasoline engine and an electric motor **4.** Coal **5.** More than five million **6.** Up to two percent **7.** 12,000 pounds (5,440 kg) **8.** Personal automated transport, or podcar

Time to Debate

Should public transportation replace cars?

Trains, subways, and buses carry millions of passengers in the United States every day. Taking public transportation to school or work is a greener form of travel than driving a car. With advances in renewable power sources, cars are becoming greener every day. However, much work lies ahead to improve green technology for cars and mass transit vehicles.

PROS

1. Total gas emissions from public transportation are less than if everyone drives cars.
2. Fewer vehicles on the road means more efficient driving.
3. Public transportation offers equal access to travel, not just for those with driver's licenses.

CONS

1. People who live in places without public transportation have no way to travel.
2. Construction of railroad and subway lines is costly.
3. Passengers have to travel according to the public transportation schedule.

WORDS TO KNOW

biofuels: renewable fuels, such as biodiesel and bioethanol, that come from organic material, including corn, sugarcane, vegetable oil, or animal fat

carbon dioxide: a greenhouse gas produced from the burning of fossil fuels, such as gasoline or diesel

carbon footprint: a measure of greenhouse gases produced by human activities

carbon offsets: credits that reduce the buyer's carbon footprint by supporting green projects, such as reforestation

dirigibles: lighter-than-air aircraft, such as blimps

emissions: harmful substances discharged in the air, such as exhaust from cars

fossil fuels: fuels, such as coal, oil, or natural gas, that are formed in the earth from plant and animal remains

geothermal energy: the kind of power obtained by using heat from within Earth

global warming: an increase in Earth's average temperature that may be caused by the greenhouse effect

greenhouse gases: gases, such as carbon dioxide and methane, that trap heat when released into the atmosphere

hybrids: vehicles that combine a gasoline engine with an electric motor

hydroelectric: related to electrical power generated from the force of falling or flowing water

megajoule: a unit that measures energy exerted by a force to move an object

monorail: a rail-based transportation system that uses a single rail

podcar: a personal automated transport (PAT) for a single passenger

recycle: to process used or waste material so that it can be used again

reforestation: renewing forest cover by planting seeds or trees

renewable: referring to a source of energy that cannot be used up, such as solar or wind energy

sustainability: the careful use of natural resources so they are not used up or permanently damaged

INDEX

Log on to www.av2books.com

AV² by Weigl brings you media enhanced books that support active learning. G
to **www.av2books.com**, and enter the special code inside the front cover of th
book. You will gain access to enriched and enhanced content that supplements
and complements this book. Content includes video, audio, web links, quizzes,
a slide show, and activities.

Audio
Listen to sections of
the book read aloud.

Video
Watch informative video clip

Web Link
Find research sites and
play interactive games.

Try This!
Complete activities and
hands-on experiments.

WHAT'S ONLINE?

Try This! Complete activities and hands-on experiments.	**Web Link** Find research sites and play interactive games.	**Video** Watch informative video clips.	**EXTRA FEATUR**
Pages 12-13 Try this activity about using greener fuels.	**Pages 8-9** Learn more about green cars.	**Pages 4-5** Watch a video about traveling green.	 **Audio** Hear introduct at the top of e
Pages 16-17 Complete an activity about making green travel plans.	**Pages 10-11** Link to more information about other kinds of green vehicles.	**Pages 14-15** View a video about mass transit.	**Key Words** Study vocabulary, and play a matching word game.
Pages 26-27 Test your knowledge of green travel.	**Pages 14-15** Find out more about mass transit.	**Pages 20-21** Learn more about green destinations.	**Slide Show** View images and captions, and try a writing activity.
Pages 30 Complete the activity in the book, and then try creating your own debate.	**Pages 28-29** Learn more about green careers.		**AV² Quiz** Take this quiz to test your knowledge